Fast Cars

How To Draw Guide

Drawing Inpiration

Aston Martin One-77

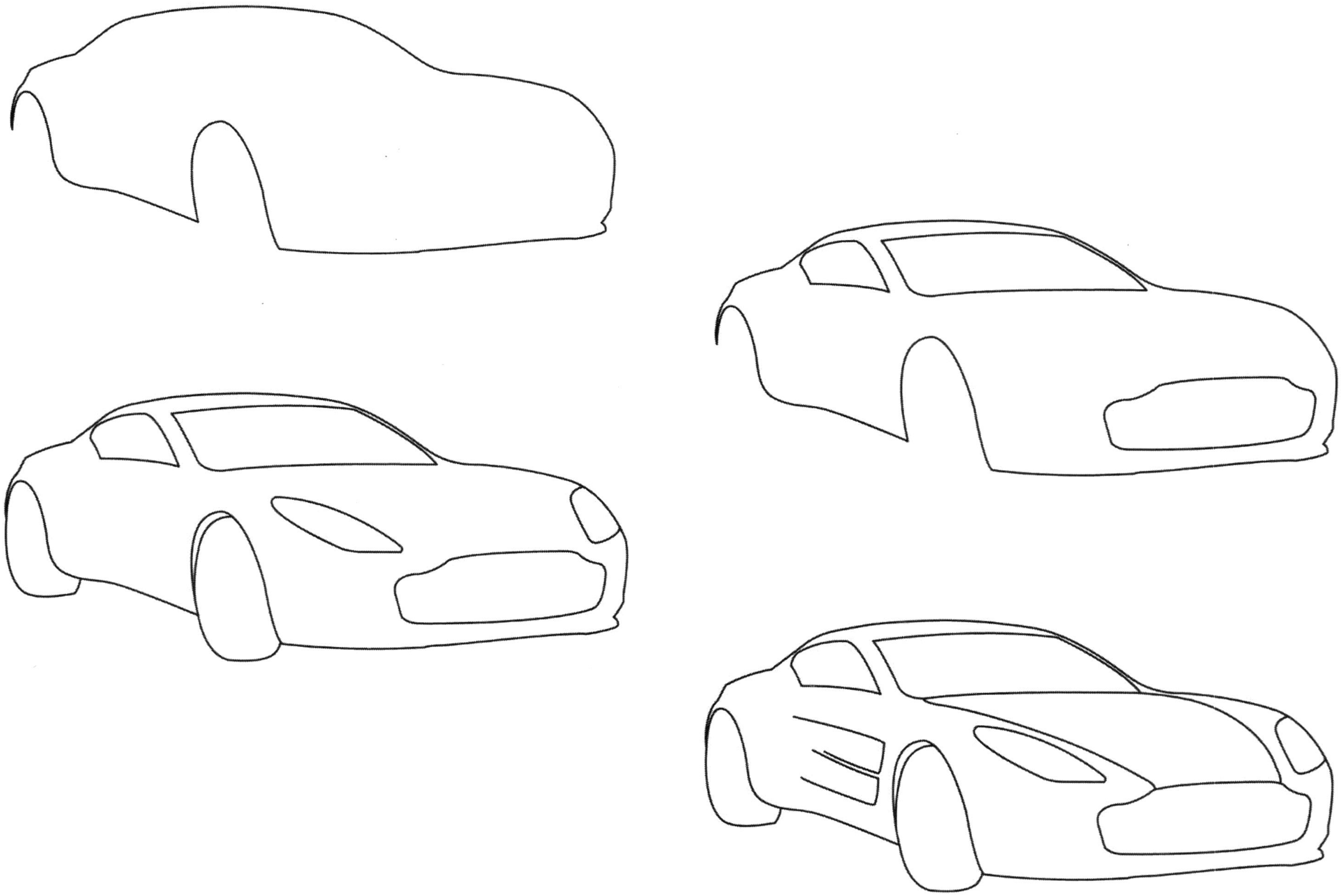

Practice Page

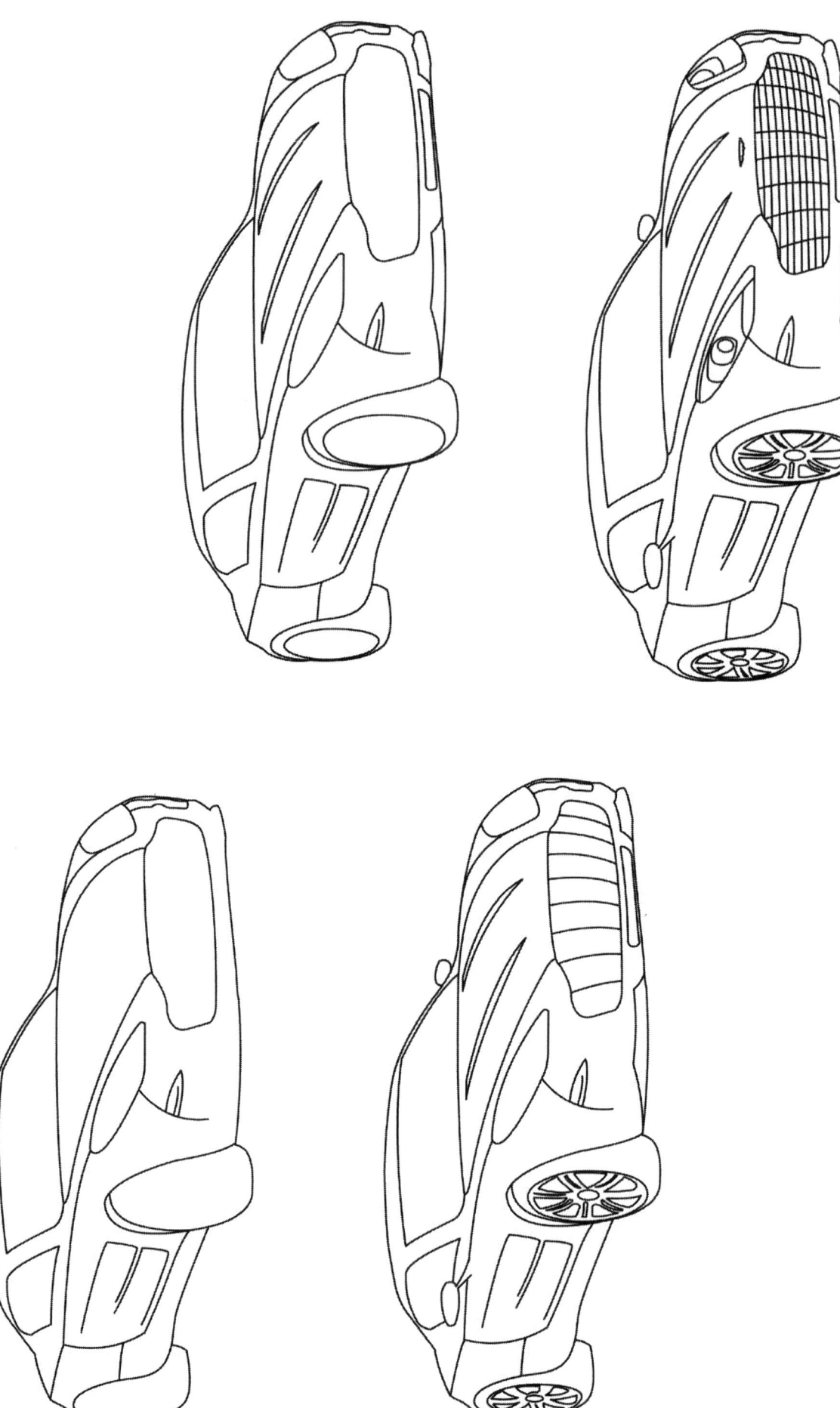

Aston Martin One-77

Practice Page

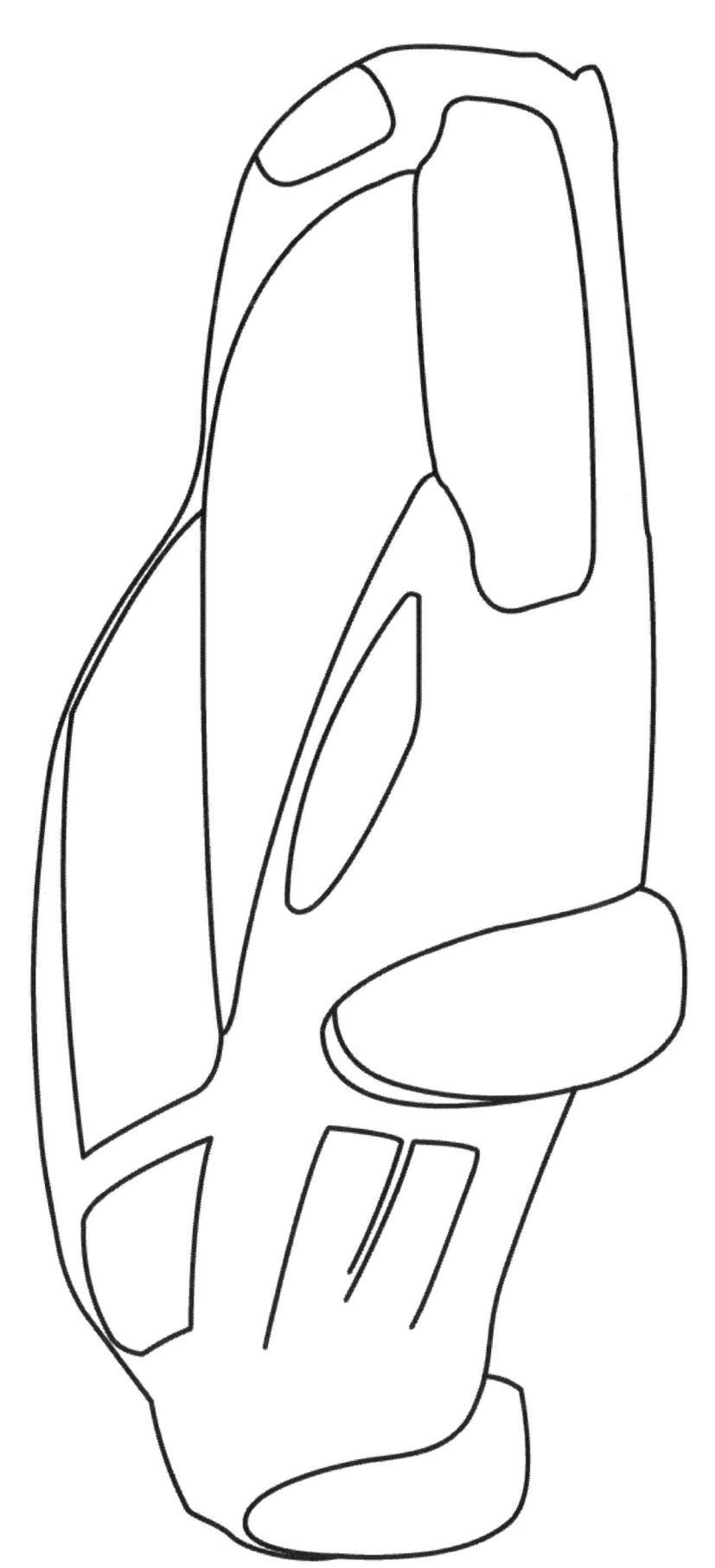

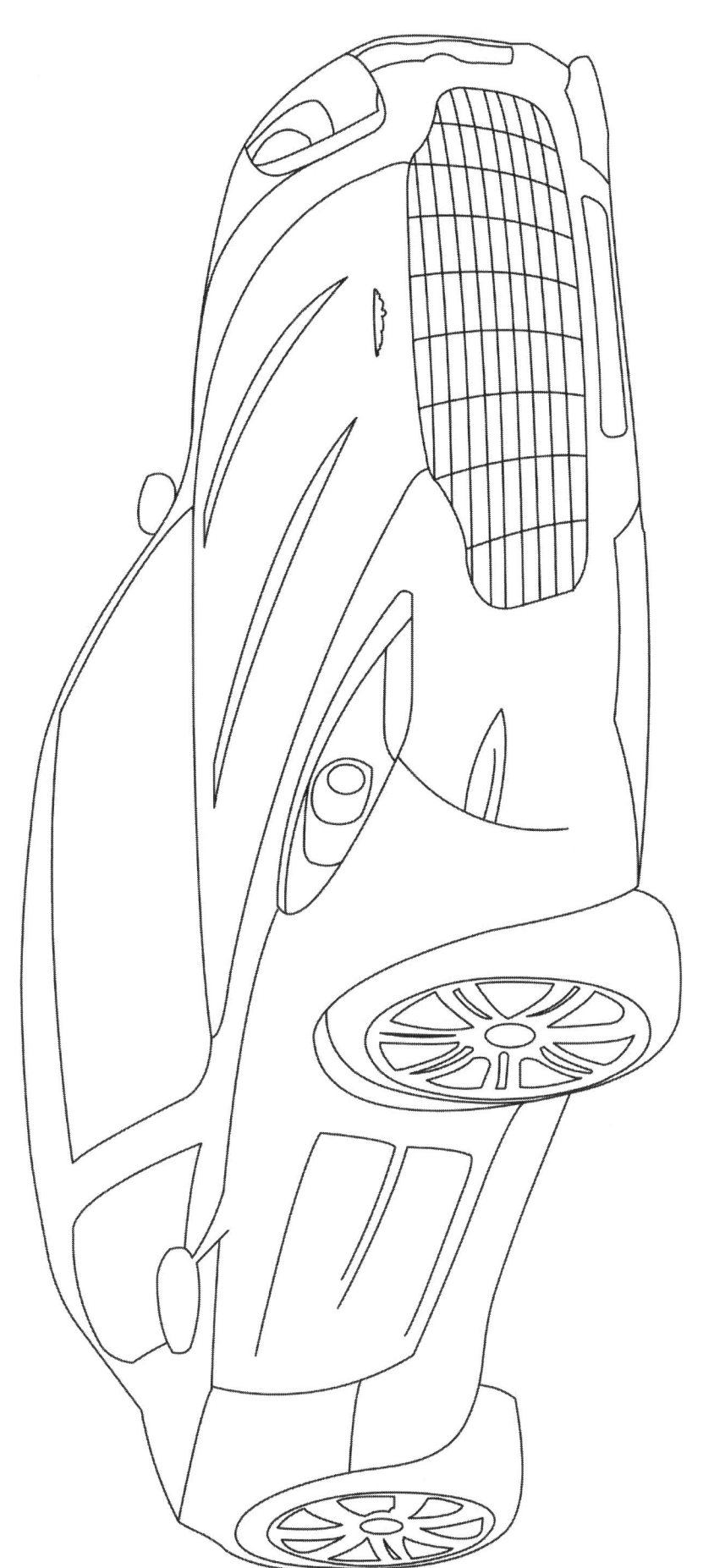

Happy Coloring!

Turn over, next one!

Bugatti Veyron

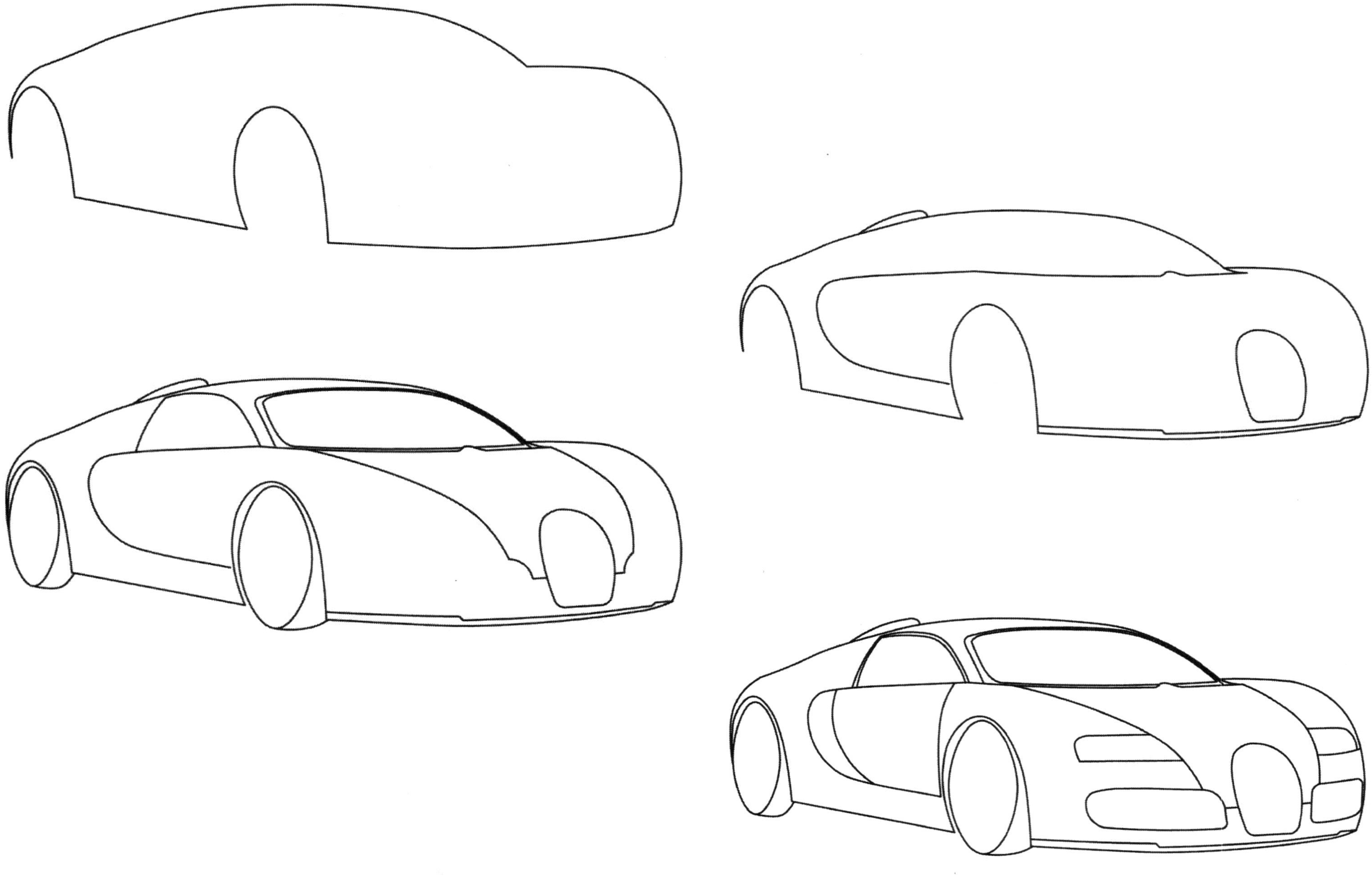

Practice Page

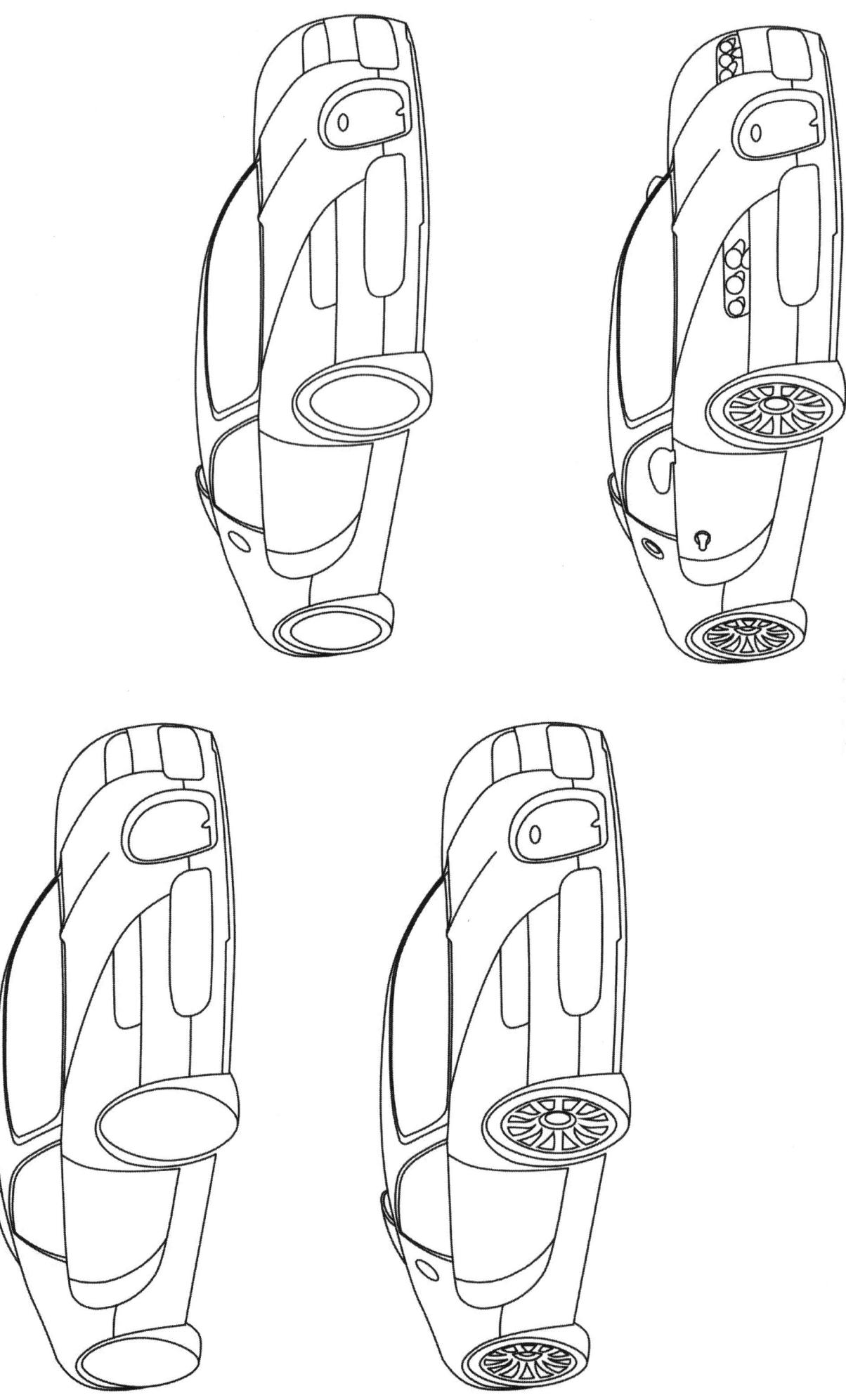

Bugatti Veyron

Practice Page

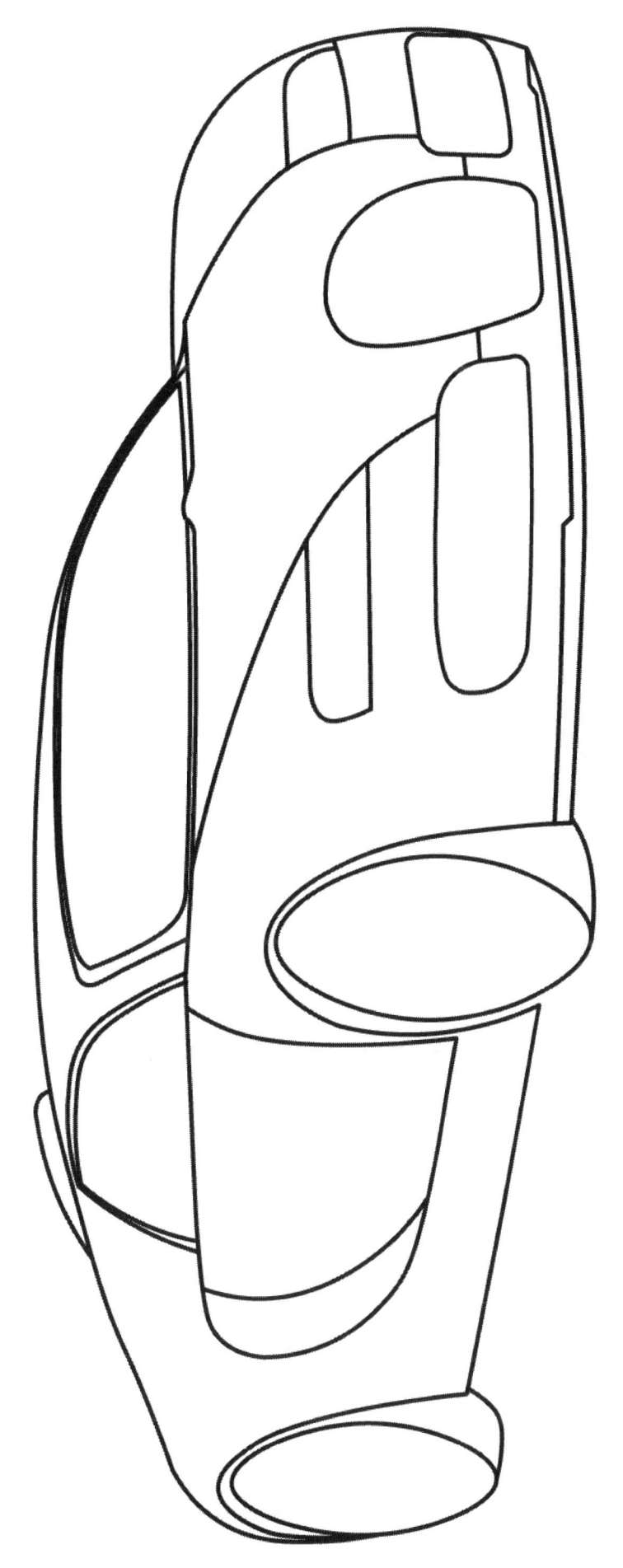

Happy Coloring!

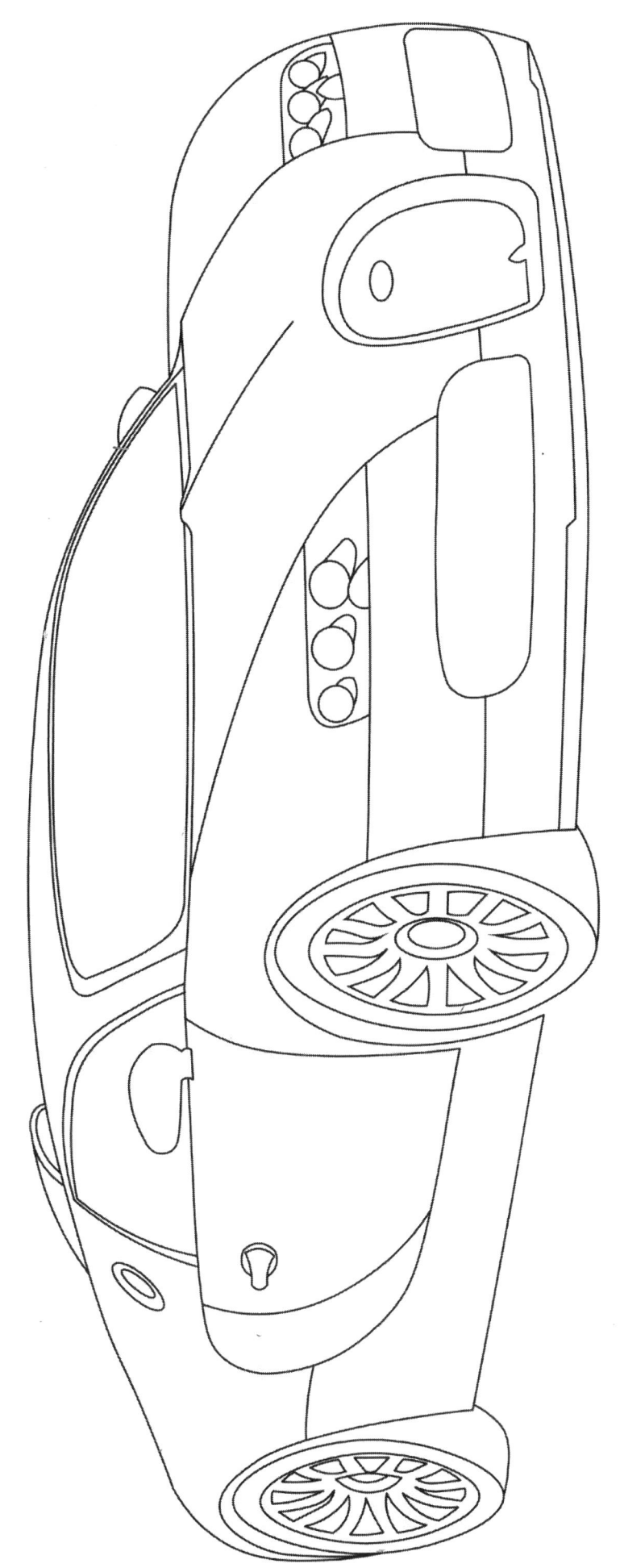

Turn over, next one!

2017 Chevrolet Camaro

Practice Page

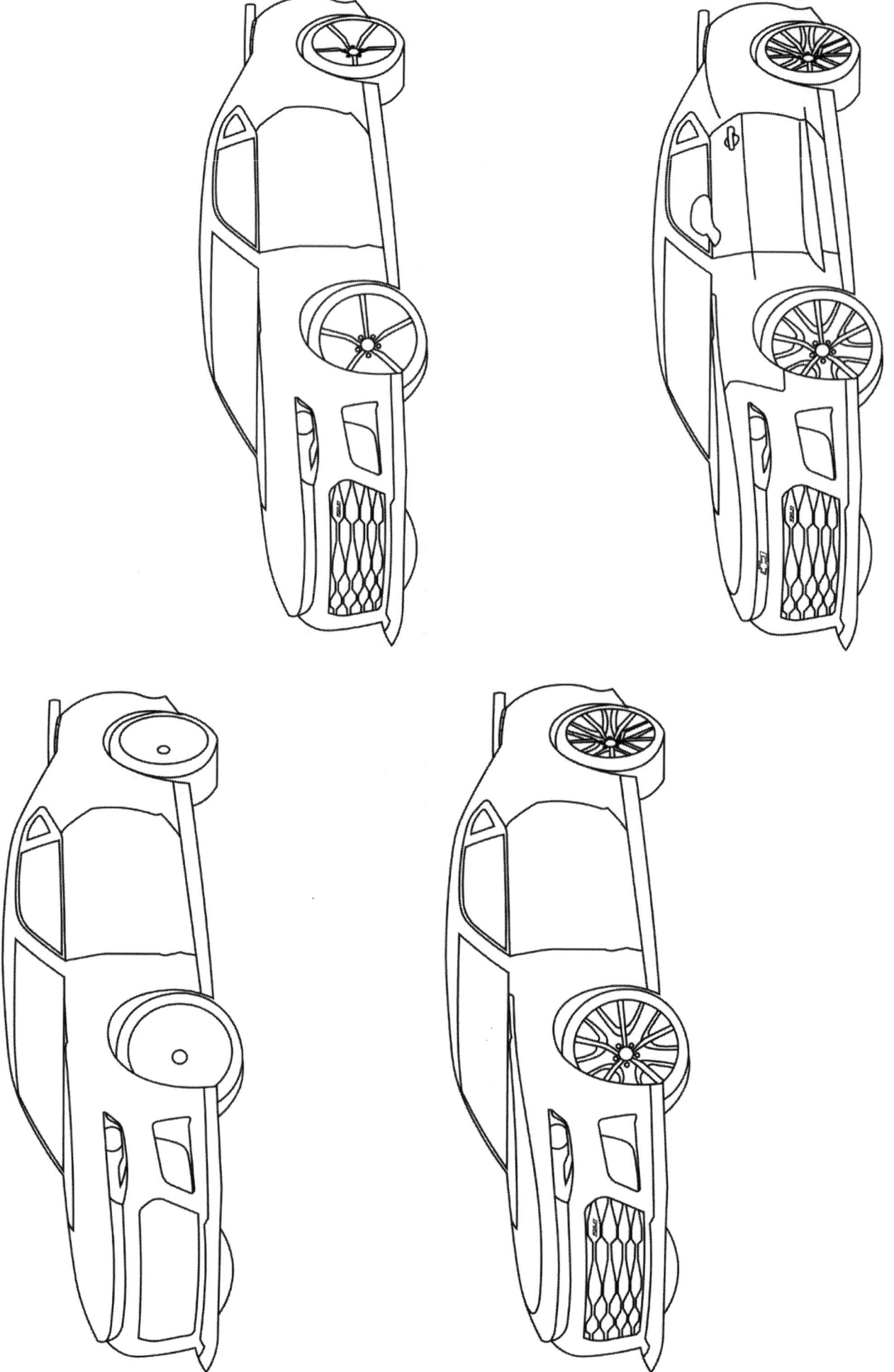

2017 Chevrolet Camaro

Practice Page

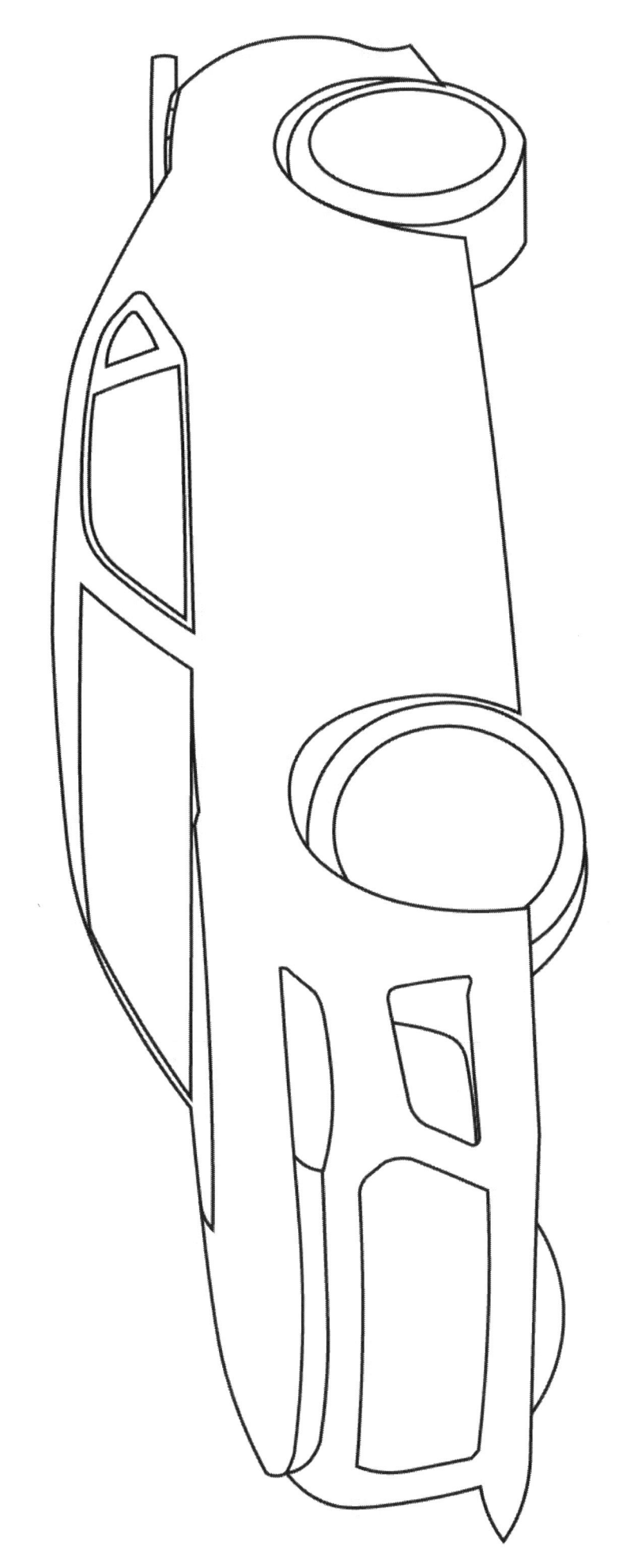

Happy Coloring!

Turn over,

next one!

2017 Dodge Challenger

Practice Page

2017 Dodge Challenger

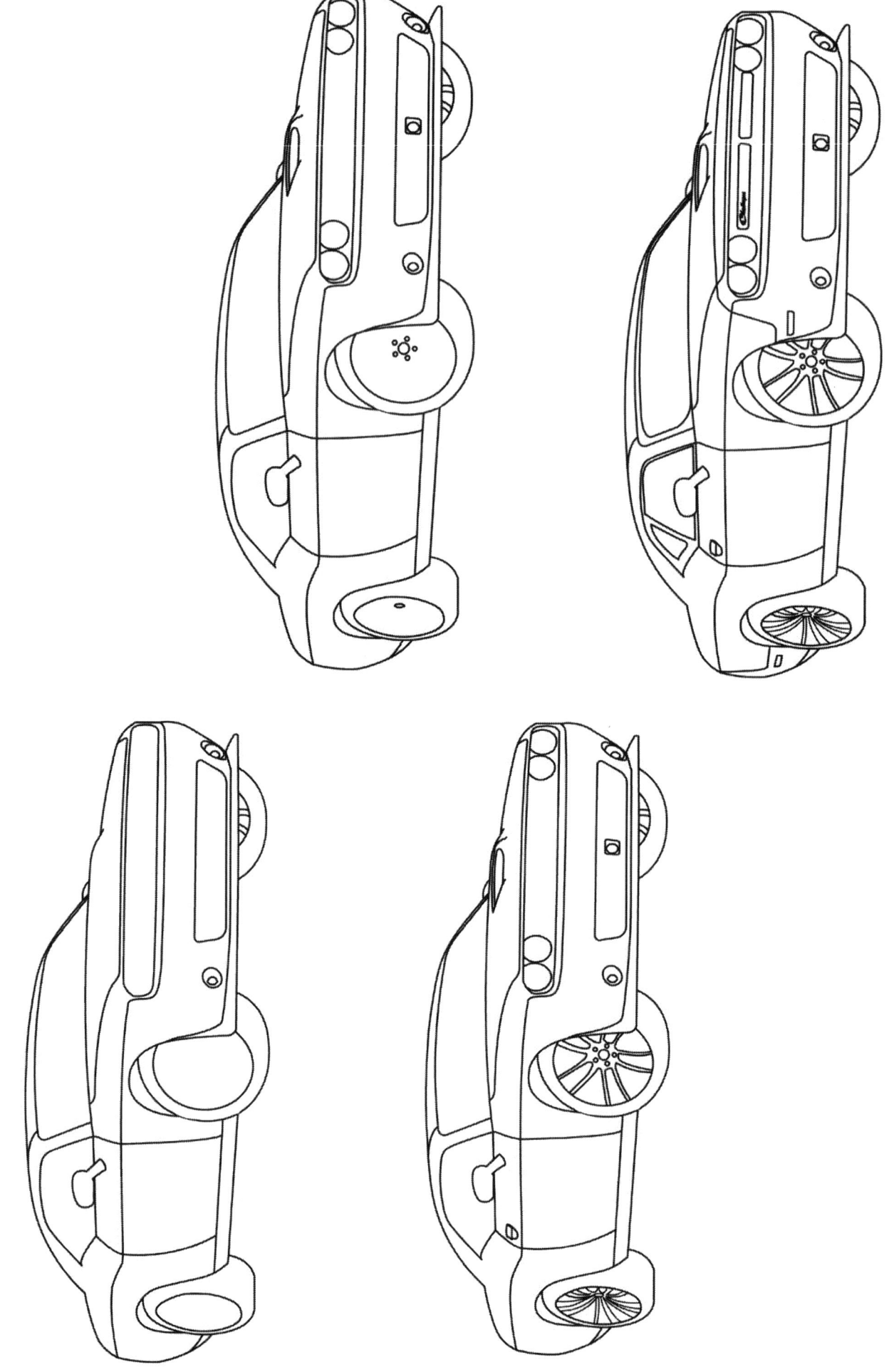

Practice Page

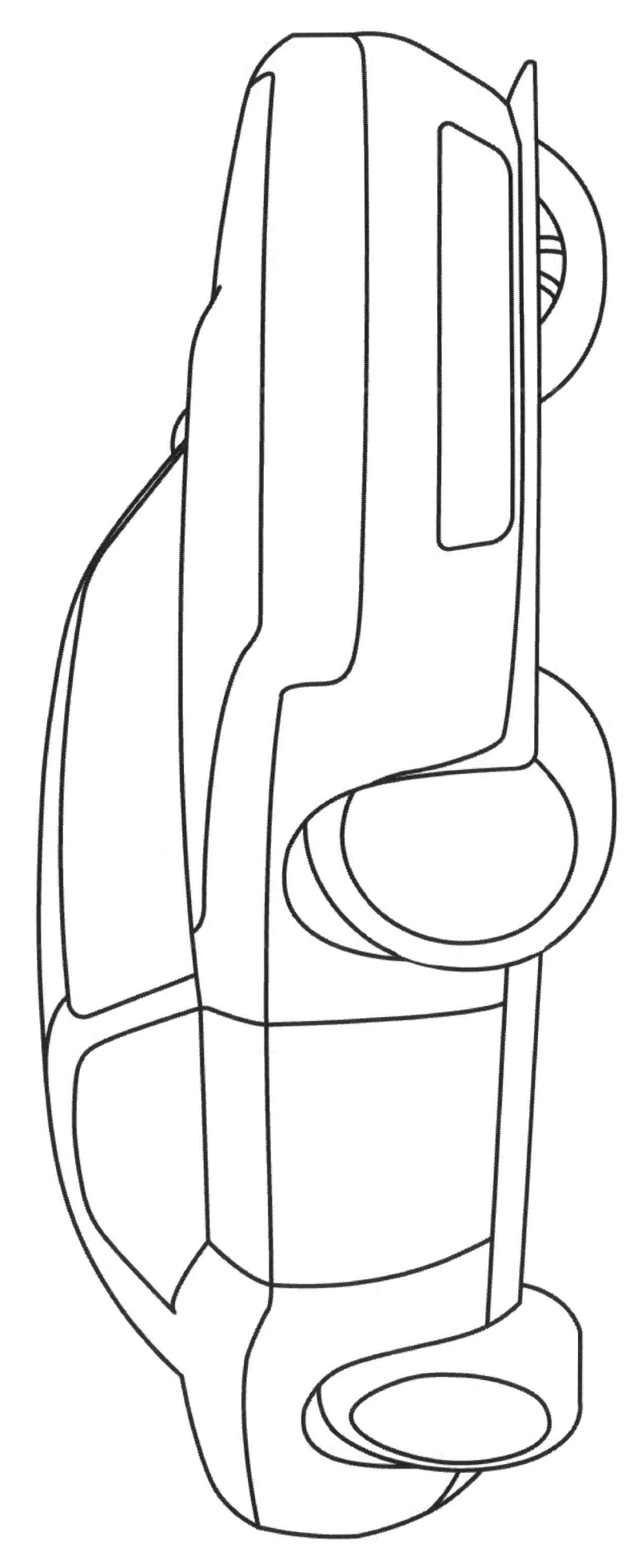

Happy Coloring!

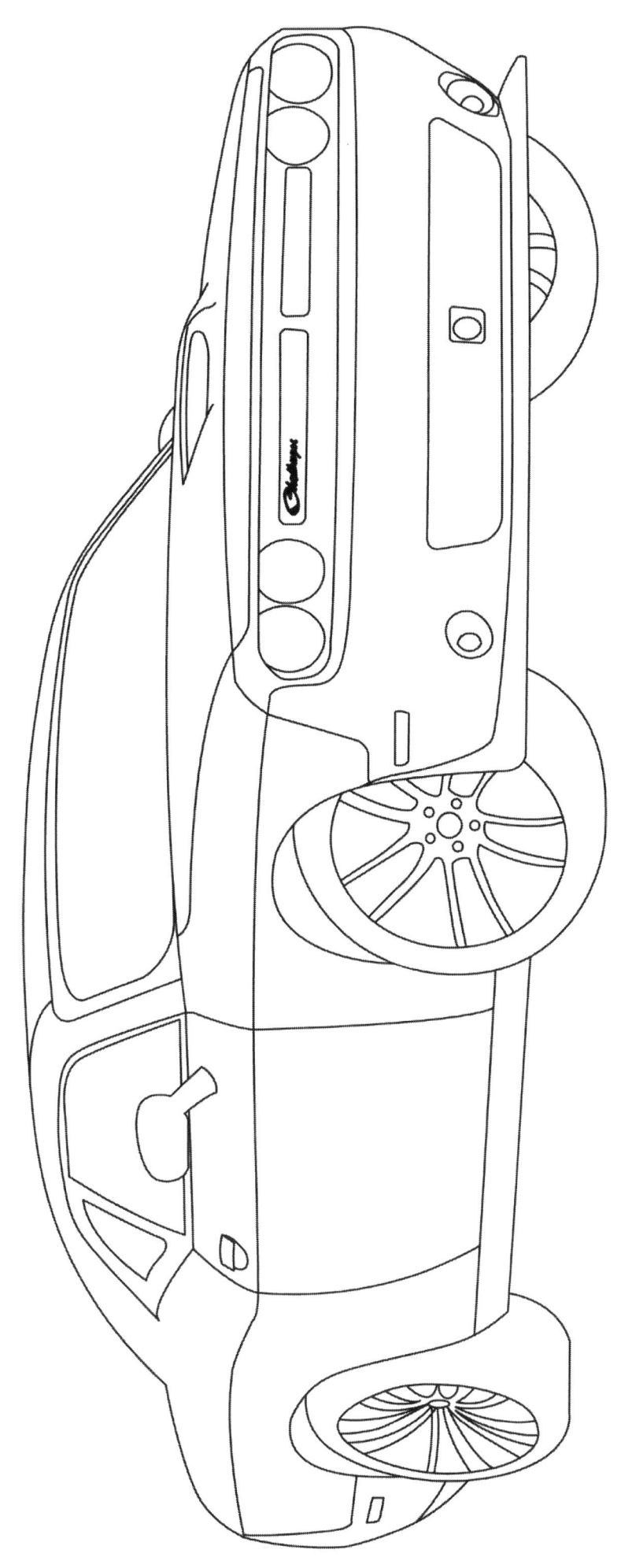

Turn over,

next one!

Ferrari Enzo

Practice Page

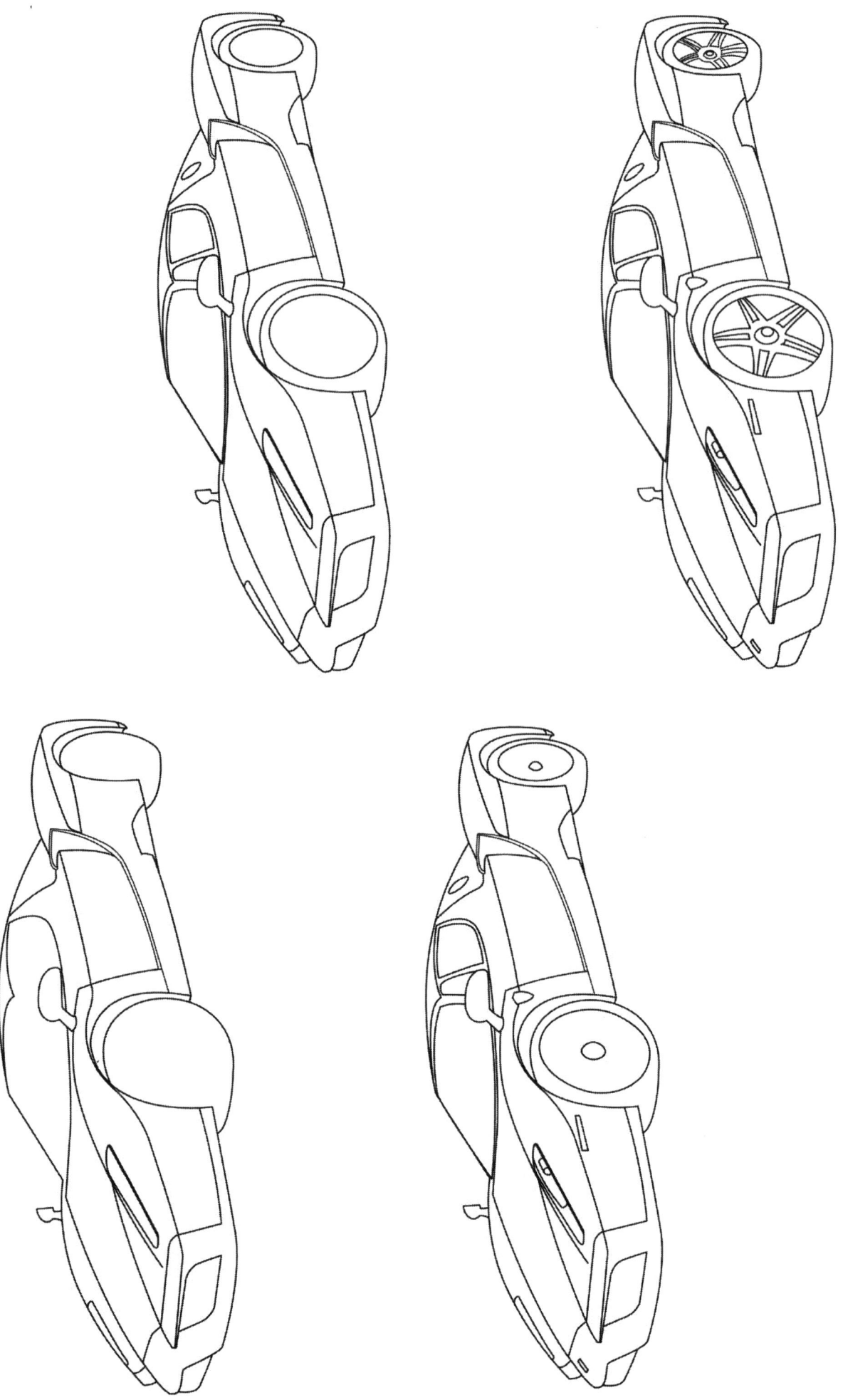

Ferrari Enzo

Practice Page

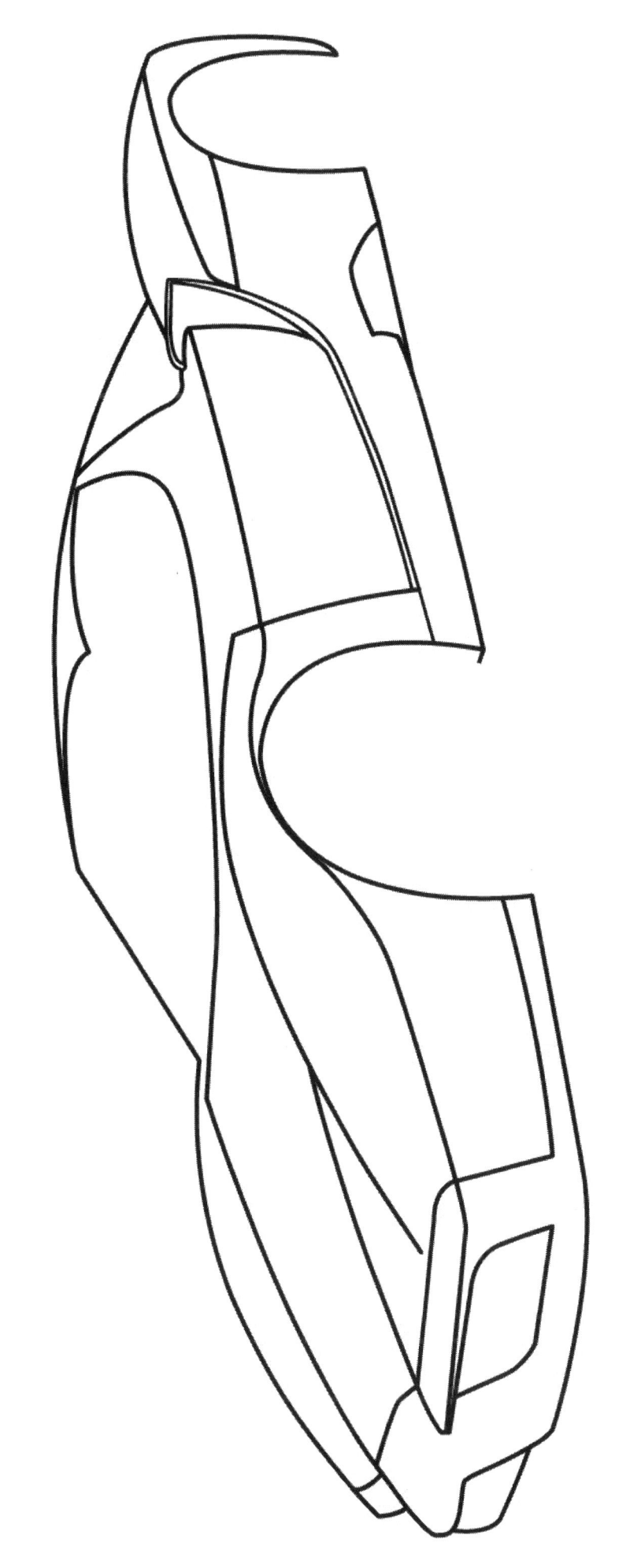

Happy Coloring!

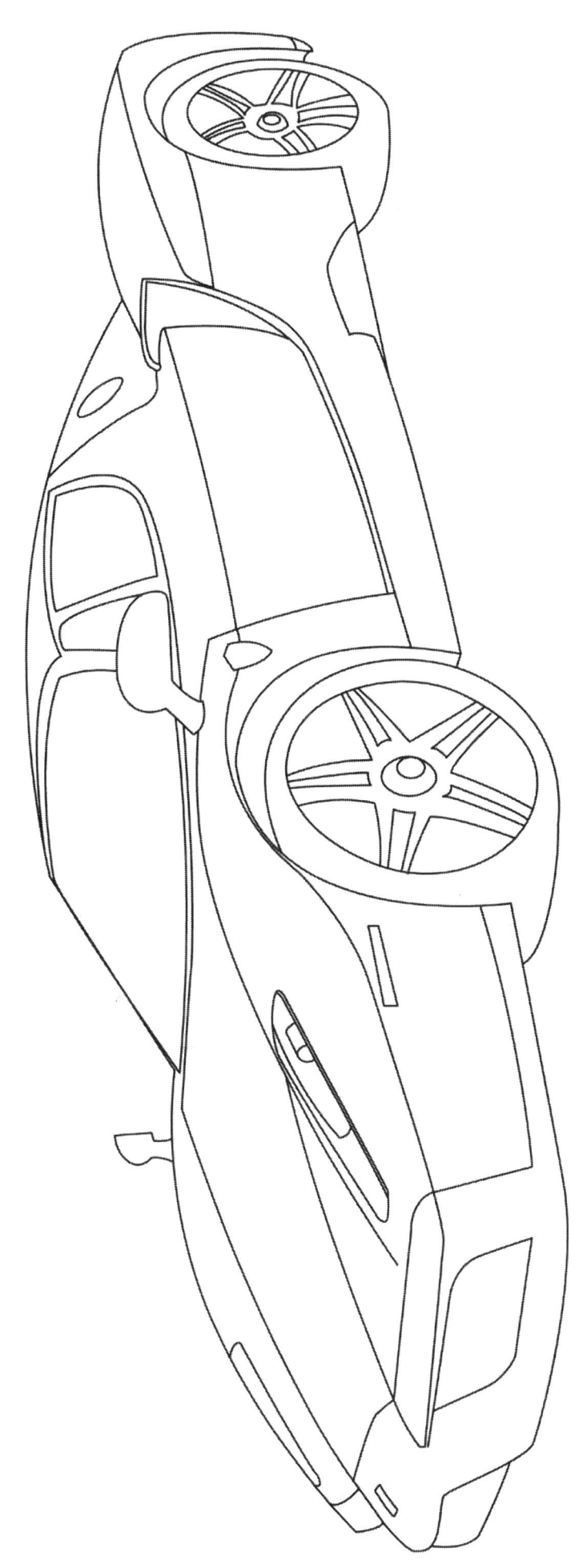

Turn over,

next one!

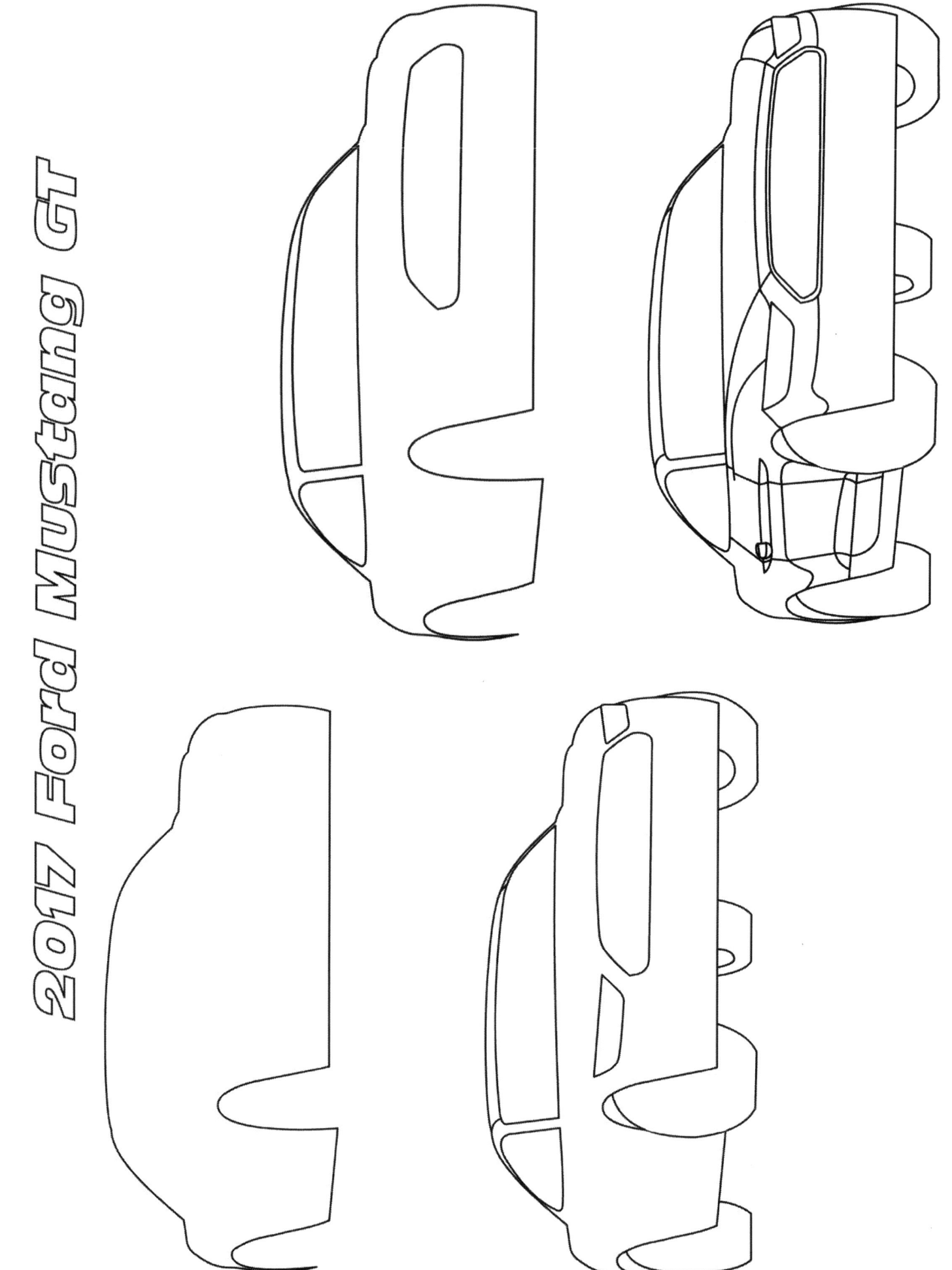

2017 Ford Mustang GT

Practice Page

2017 Ford Mustang GT

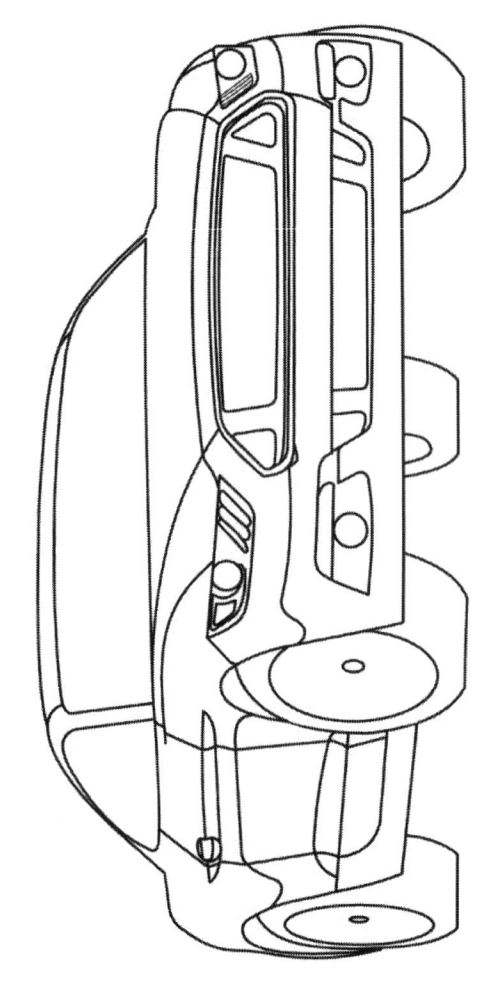

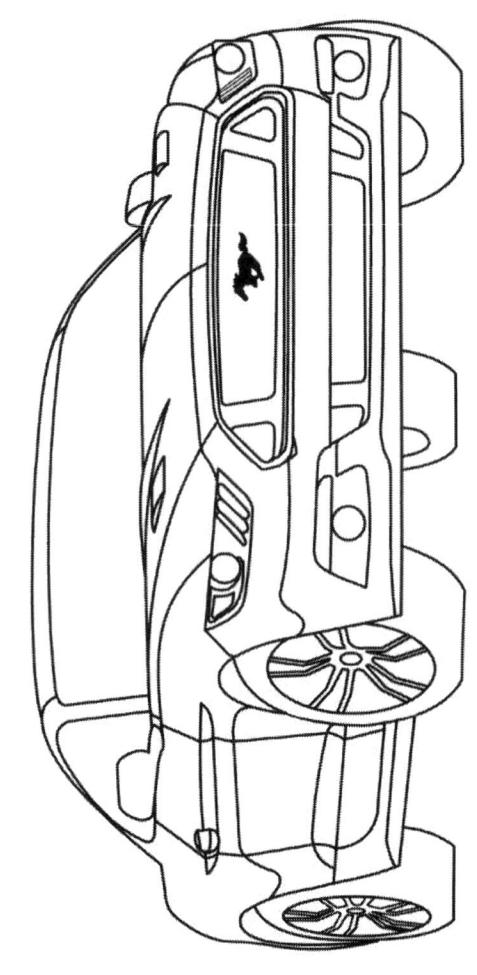

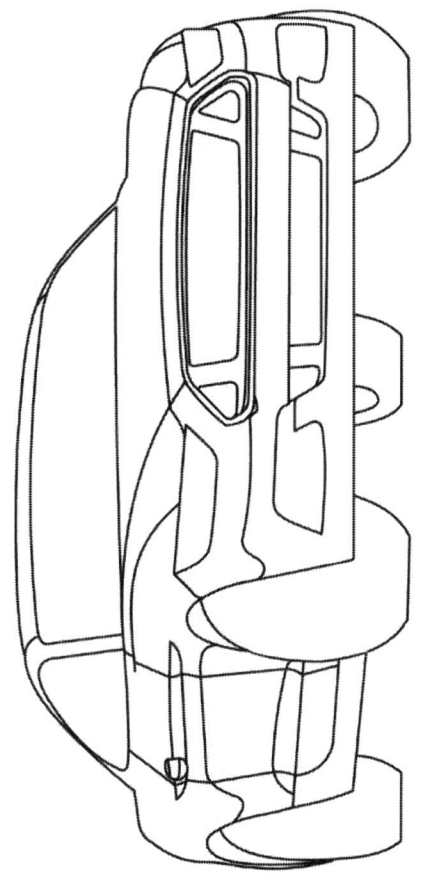

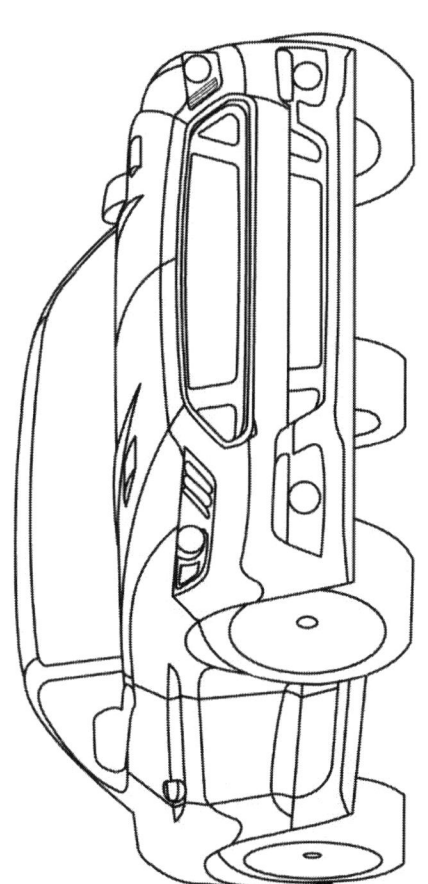

Practice Page

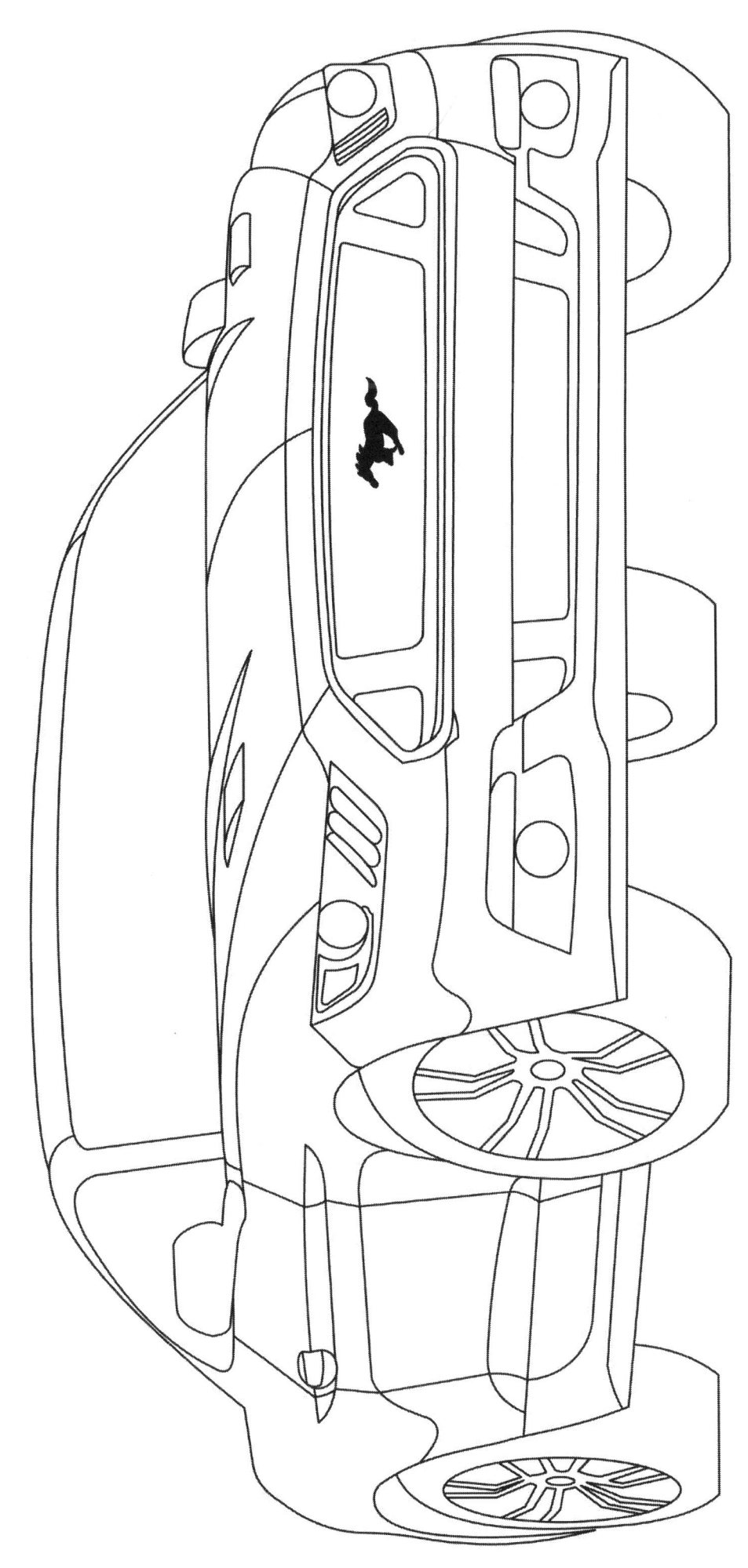

Happy Coloring!

Turn over, next one!

Koenigsegg Agera R

Practice Page

Koenigsegg Agera R

Practice Page

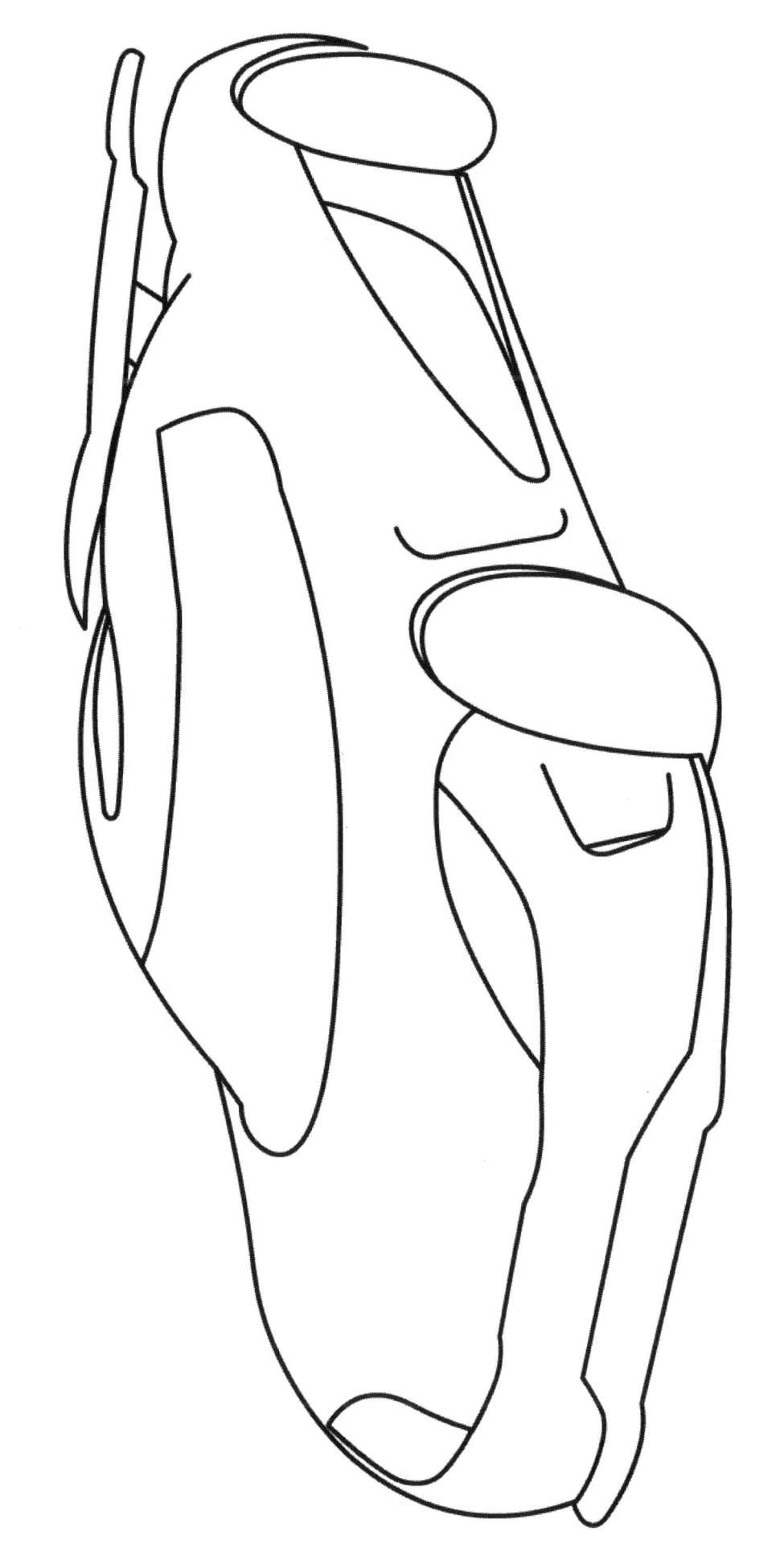

Happy Coloring!

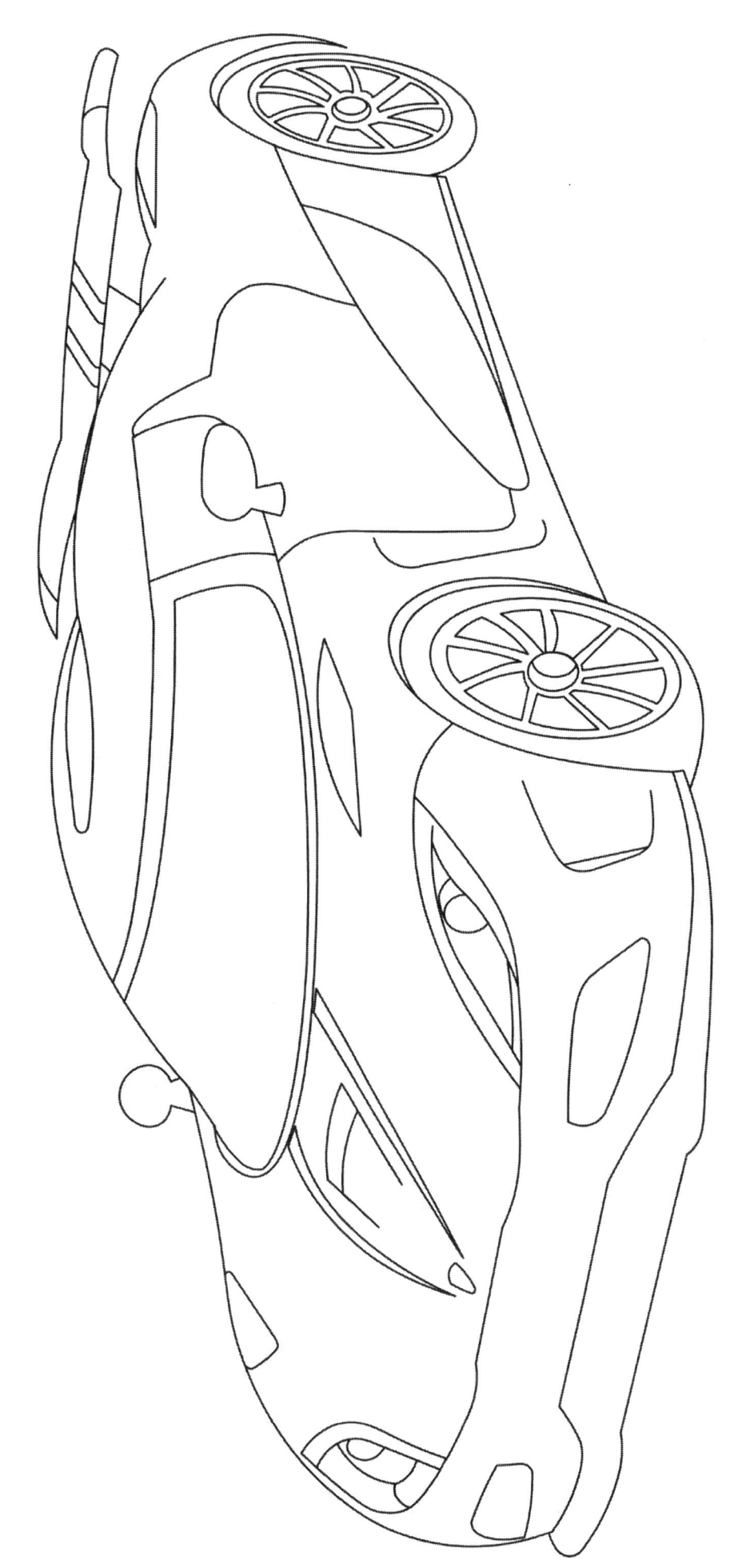

Turn over,

next one!

McLaren F1

Practice Page

McLaren F1

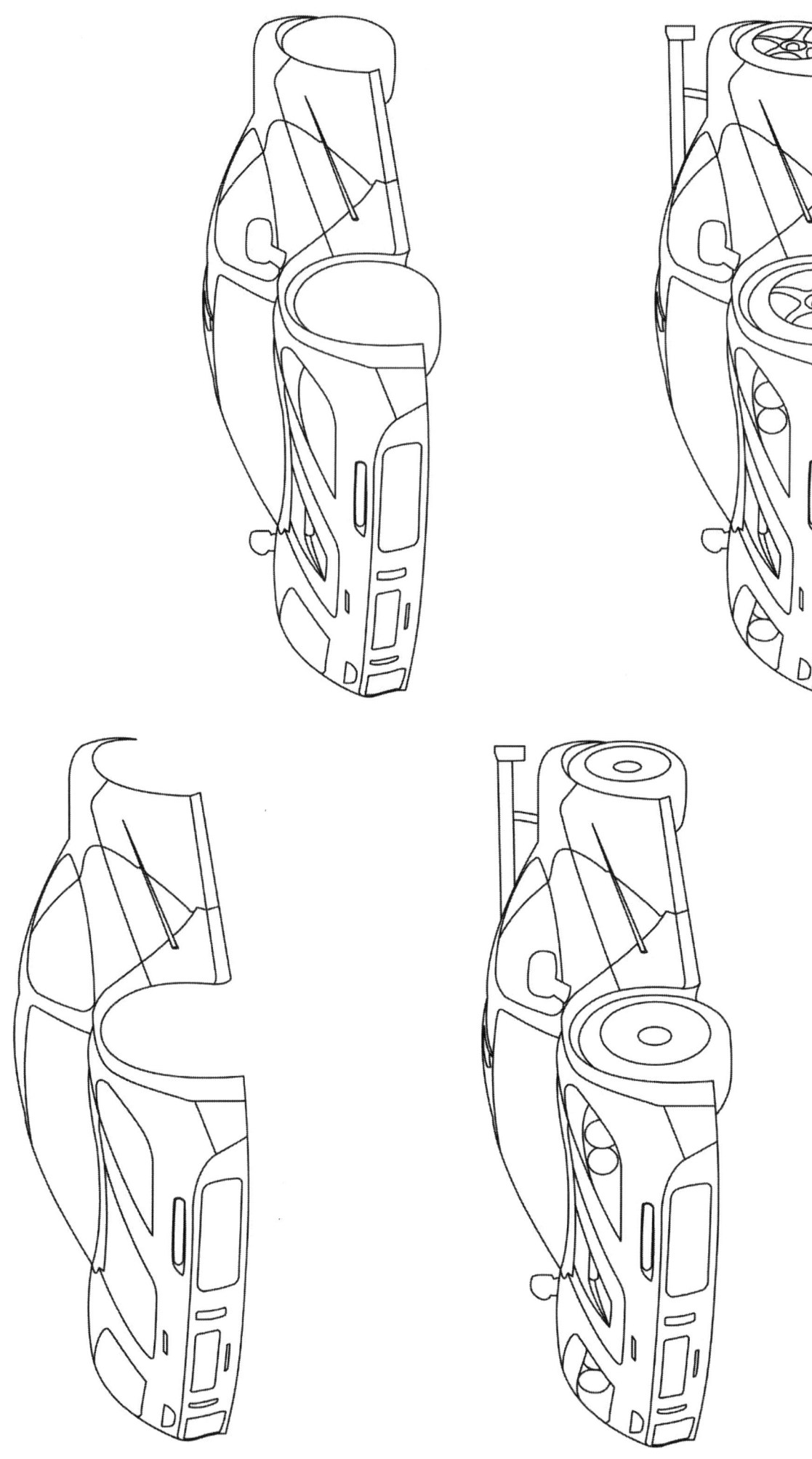

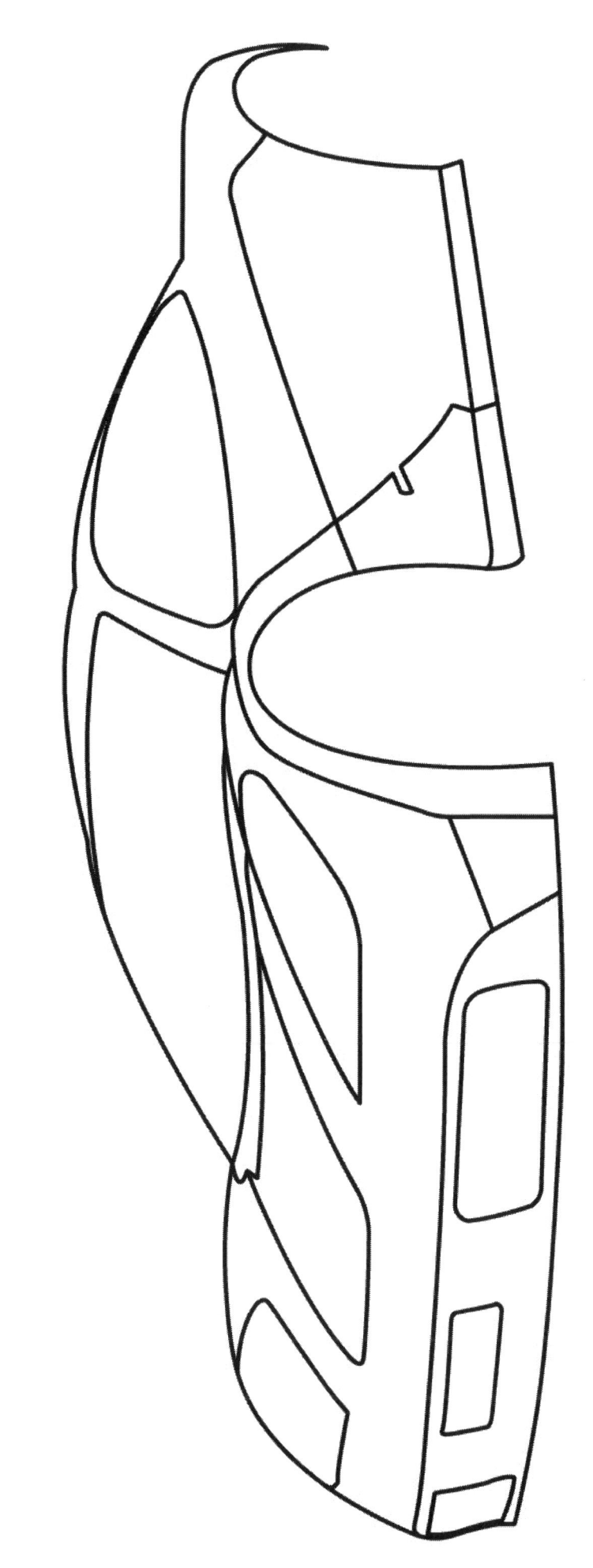

Happy coloring!

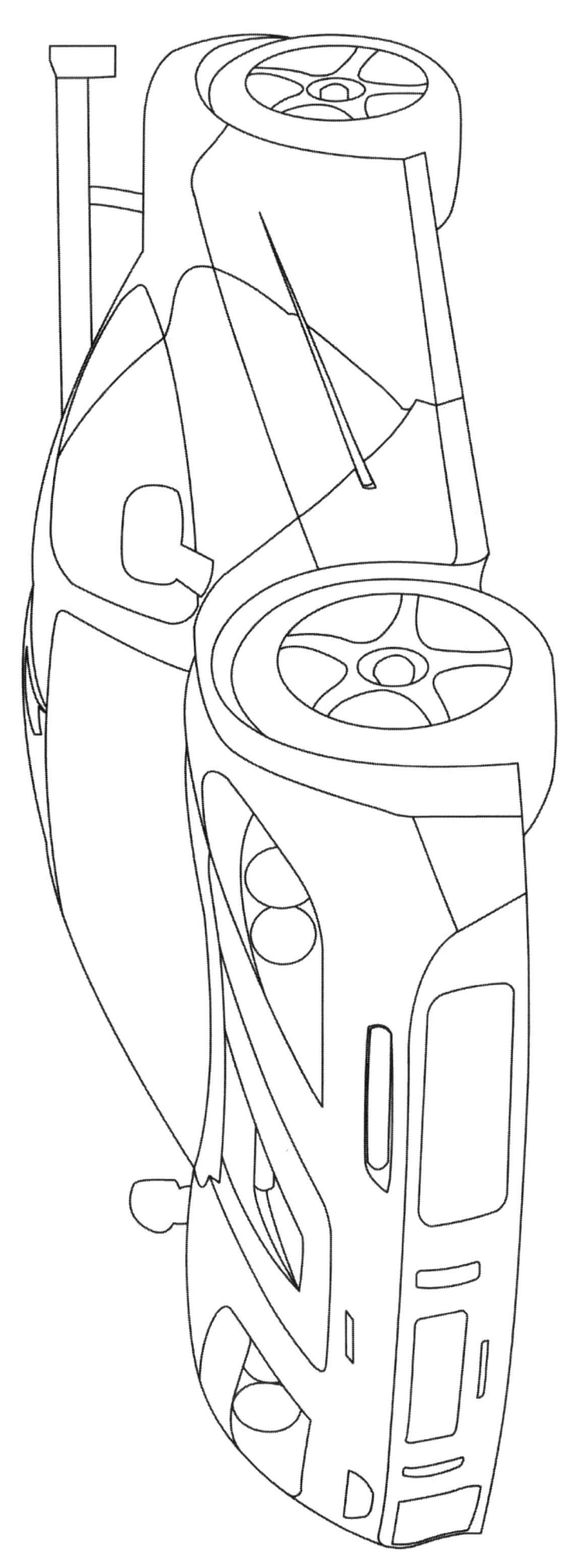

Turn over,

next one!

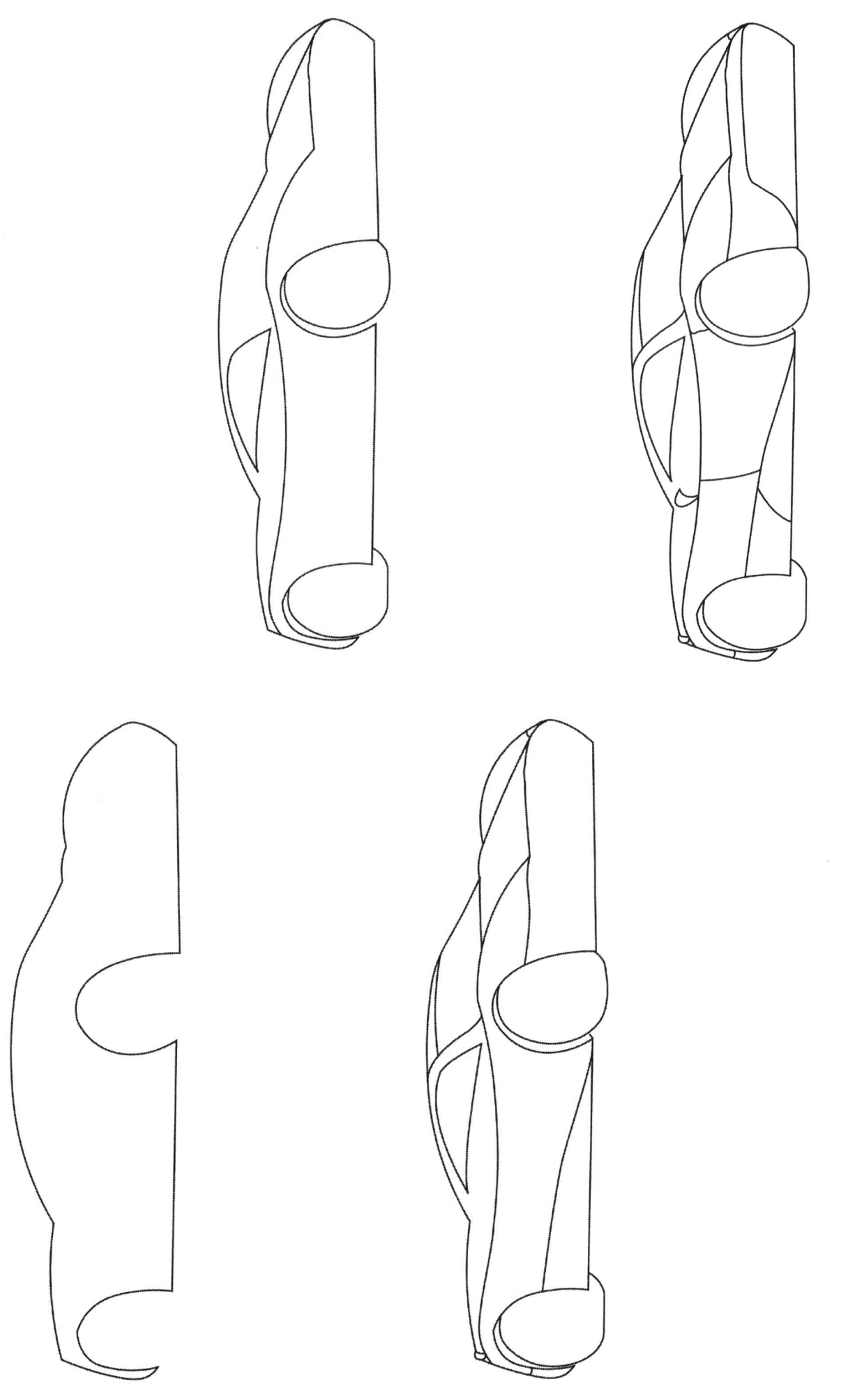

Pagani Huayra

Practice Page

Pagani Huayra

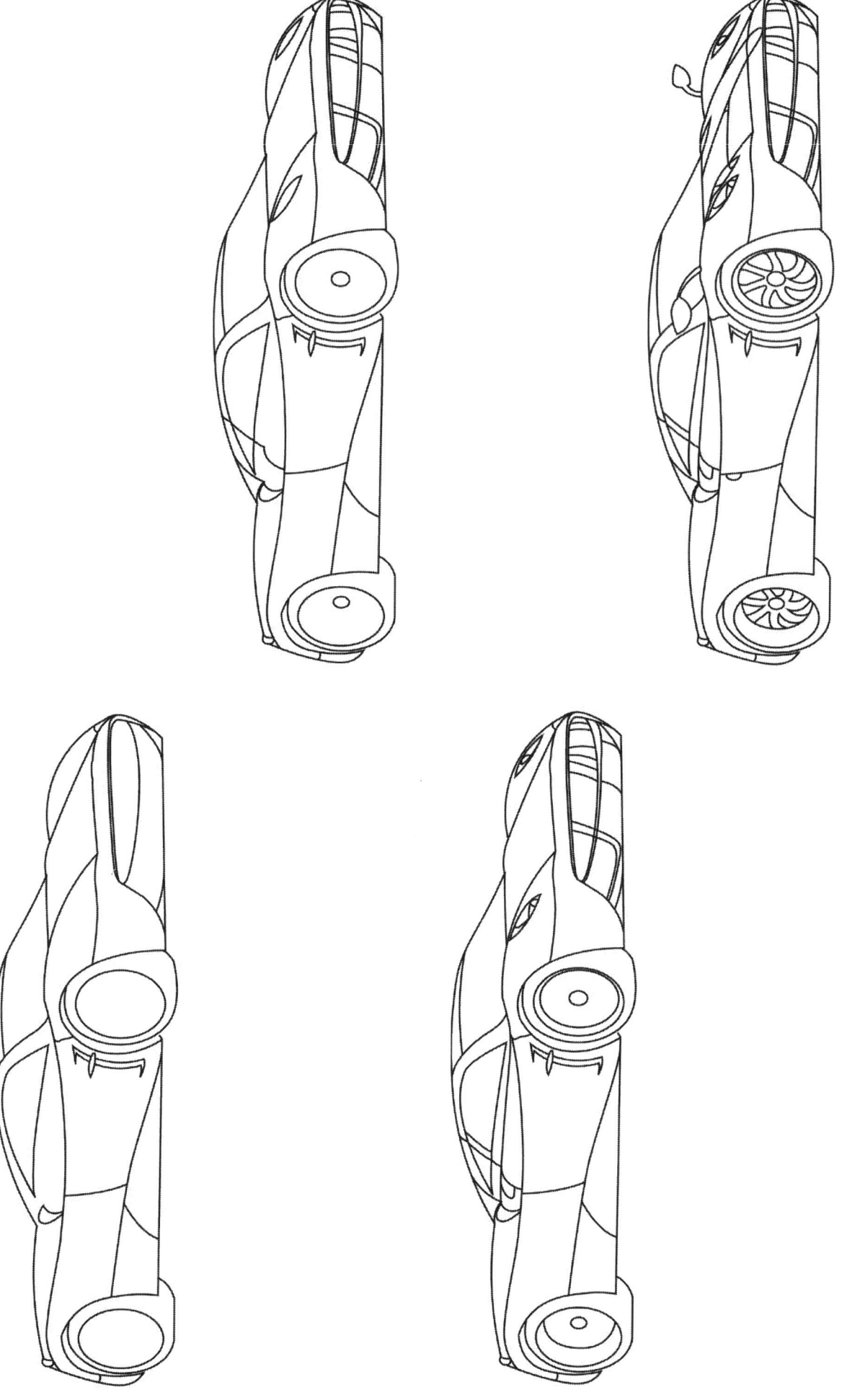

Practice Page

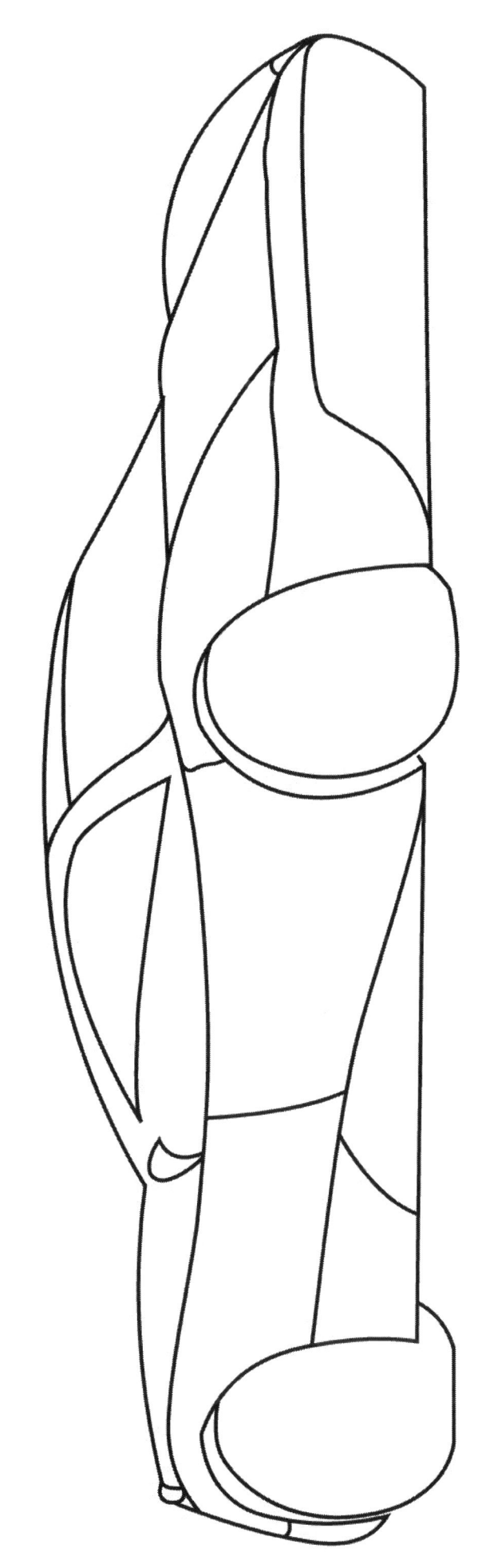

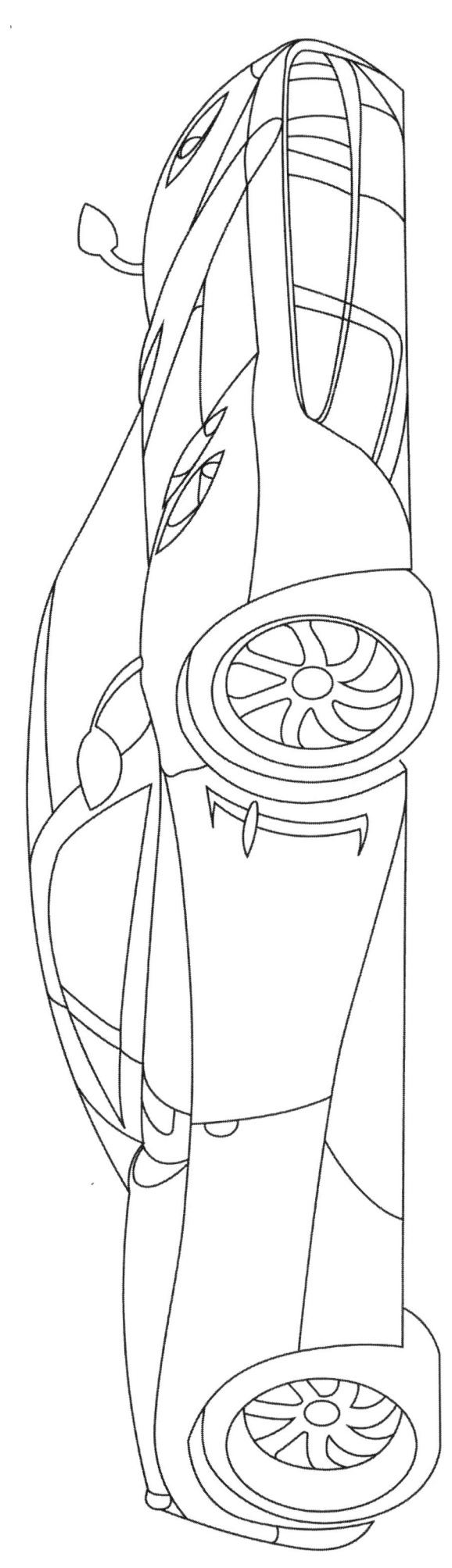

Happy Coloring!

Turn over,

next one!

Porsche GT9-R

Practice Page

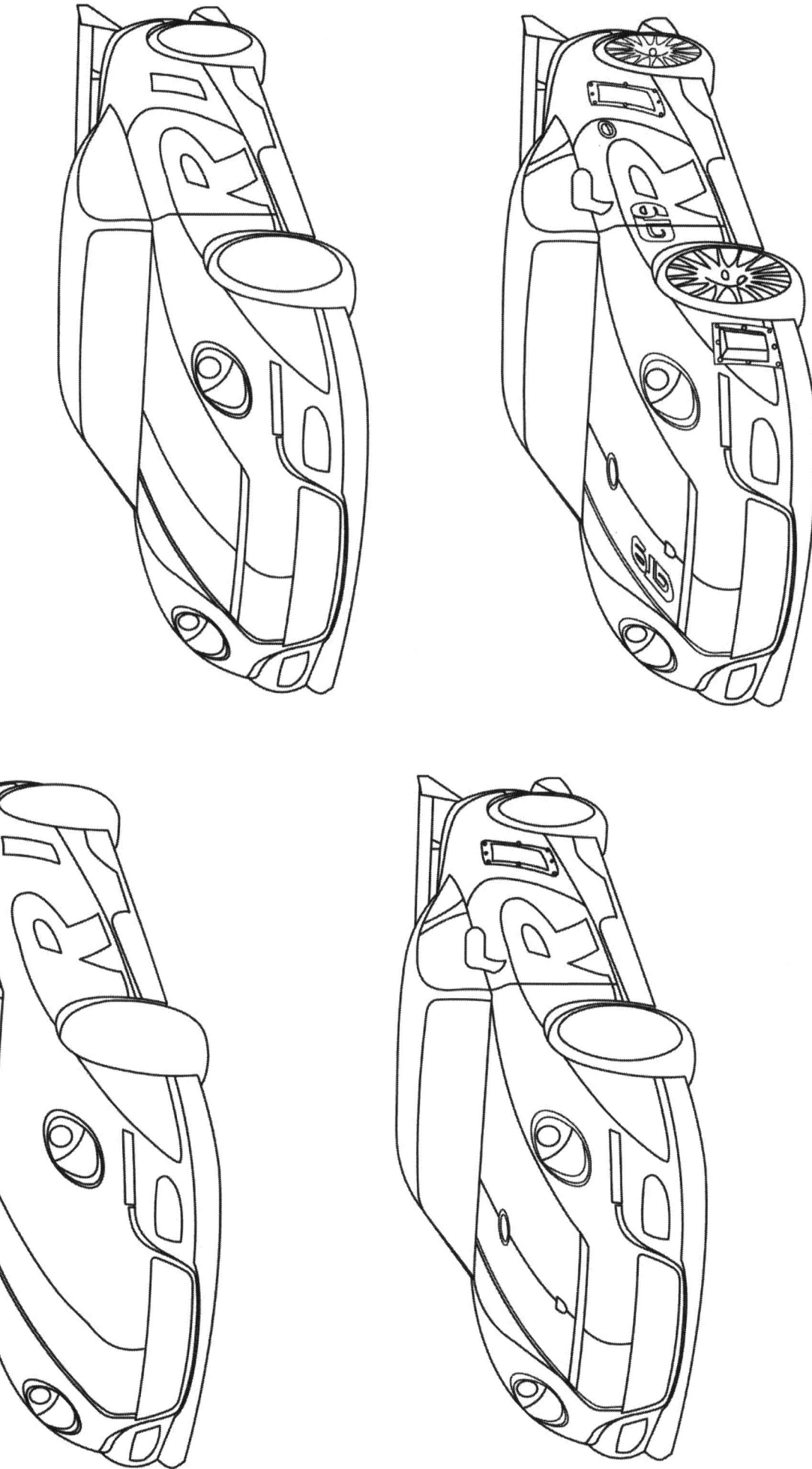

Porsche GT9-R

Practice Page

Happy Coloring!

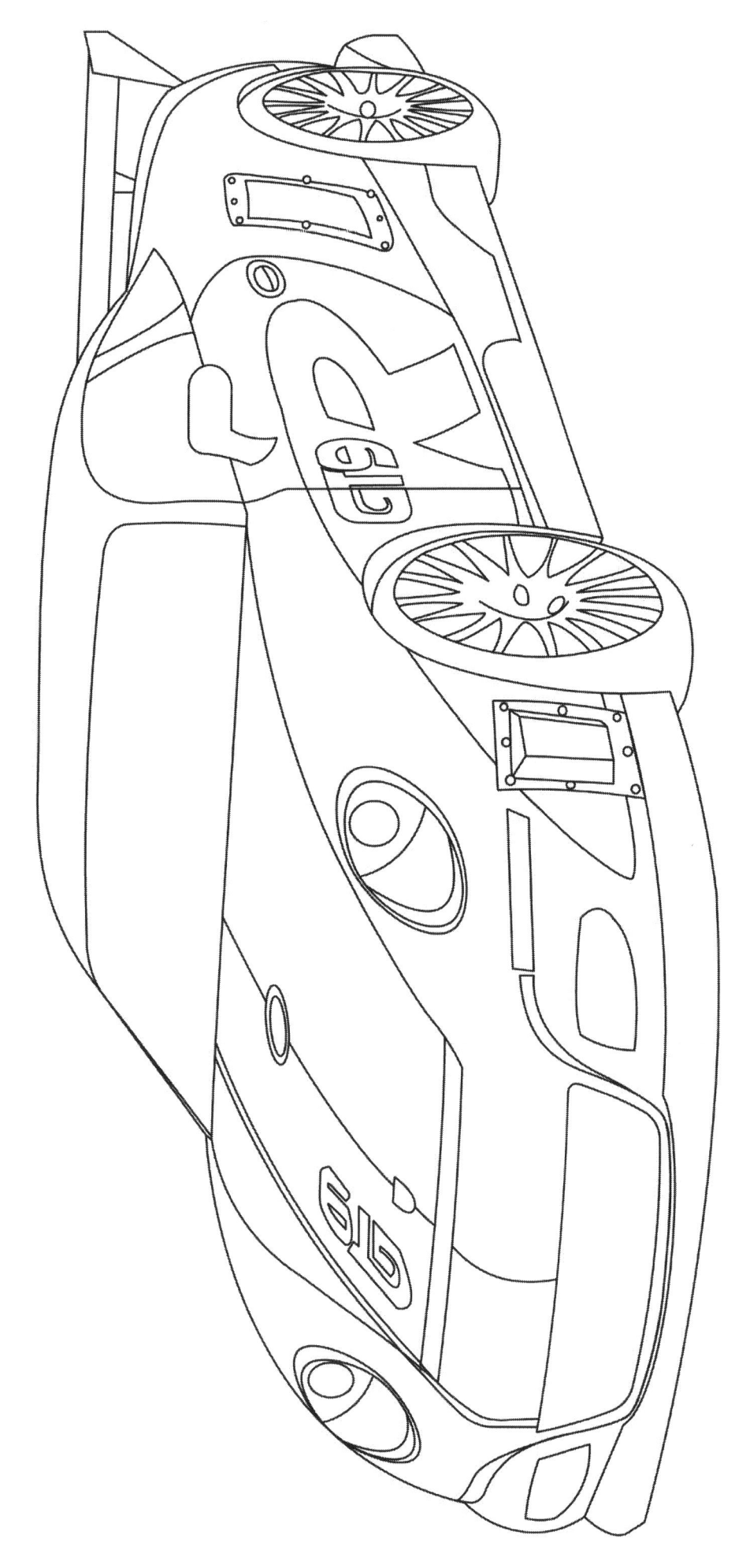

Made in the USA
Lexington, KY
02 December 2019